ALSO BY JOHN HOLLANDER

Poetry
 Picture Window 2003
 Figurehead and Other Poems 1999
 Tesserae and Other Poems 1993
 Selected Poetry 1993
 Harp Lake 1988
 In Time and Place 1986
 Powers of Thirteen 1983
 Blue Wine and Other Poems 1979
 Spectral Emanations: New and Selected Poems 1978
 Reflections on Espionage 1976
 Tales Told of the Fathers 1975
 The Head of the Bed 1974
 Town and Country Matters 1972
 The Night Mirror 1971
 Types of Shape 1969
 Visions from the Ramble 1965
 Movie-Going 1962
 A Crackling of Thorns 1958

Criticism
 The Poetry of Everyday Life 1998
 The Work of Poetry 1997
 The Gazer's Spirit 1995
 Melodious Guile: Fictive Pattern in Poetic Language 1988
 Rhyme's Reason: A Guide to English Verse 1981
 The Figure of Echo: A Mode of Allusion in Milton and After 1981
 Vision and Resonance: Two Senses of Poetic Form 1975
 The Untuning of the Sky: Ideas of Music in English Poetry 1500–1700 1961

For Children
 The Immense Parade on Supererogation Day and What Happened to It 1972
 The Quest of the Gole 1966

A DRAFT OF LIGHT

A DRAFT OF LIGHT

Poems

John Hollander

 Alfred A. Knopf   New York   2008

THIS IS A BORZOI BOOK
PUBLISHED BY ALFRED A. KNOPF

Copyright © 2008 by John Hollander

All rights reserved. Published in the United States by
Alfred A. Knopf, a division of Random House, Inc., New York, and in
Canada by Random House of Canada, Limited, Toronto.
www.aaknopf.com

Knopf, Borzoi Books, and the colophon are registered trademarks
of Random House, Inc.

Library of Congress Cataloging-in-Publication Data

Hollander, John.
A draft of light : poems / by John Hollander.—1st ed.
p. cm.
Includes bibliographical references.
ISBN 978-0-307-26911-9
I. Title.
PS3515.O3485D73 2008
811'.54—dc22   2008004751

Manufactured in the United States of America
First Edition

Again, for Natalie

Contents

HAUNTINGS

The Outcasts	3
A Ghost Story	4
Ghosts	6
The Sparklers	8
Glimpse of a Silence	9
Jane	11
What's on the Wall	13
Very Early	16
Traces	17
Out of Sight, Still in Mind	19
Undecipherable Ms. Found in a Time Capsule	21
Policing the Yard	23

TALES AND FABLES

Monday Morning	27
A Ballad Romantically Restored	29
A Draft of Light	34
Setting Out for the Inner as the Outer Sets In	36
Steep Declension	37
Attic Nights	39
Being Stung by a Bee on the Lexington Avenue Local	45
Stationary Bicycle	48
When We Went Up	51
Dr. Johnson's Fable	54
Typing Lesson: A Little Fable	55
Getting It Right	57
From the Notes of a Traveler	58

FIDDLING AROUND

Emeritus Faculties	63
Fiddle-Faddle	64
For "Fiddle-De-Dee"	66
No Fiddling	68
Second Fiddle	69
First Music Lesson	71
Another Cause for Wonder	73
Marine Tongue Twister	74
Old Saws Newly Sharpened	75
Missing Coordinates	77
Still and Yet	78
A Confession	79
Fidget	80

FURTHER ESSAYS

Prosaic Translation	83
Fifty Years Ago	85
Rooting for the Yankees	86
Some Playthings	92
Pretty as a Picture	94
Meditation on a Lawn	95
Weather Report	96
At the Year's End	98
The Way It All Goes On	99
Question About an Old Question	101
By Nature	103
Notes	107
Acknowledgments	109

HAUNTINGS

THE OUTCASTS

She had once heard tell
Of what sometimes could be seen
    In only the most
Healthy and ordinary
Open places in daylight:

Shadows wandering
Ghostlike through the visible
    World, detached, flatly,
Darkly and despairingly
In search of the substances

—Active themselves or
Motionless—which had cast them
    On whatever it
Was they had been flung across
When newly born? Or, longing

To rejoin not their
Hard mothering bodies but
    The fathering light
Occluded, creating the voids
Out of which shadows are shaped?

Later on in life
She would fall to wondering
    Whether she had been
Spared this sight, and what it must
Mean, or been deprived of it.

A GHOST STORY

Shadows are the ghosts
Of the bodies—animal
Vegetable or

Mineral—that can
Cast them, thought the child.
But that didn't work

Too well with her lore
About how ghosts were diseased
Souls wailing for health,

And how they outlived
The bodies that housed them (but
When inside those homes

Couldn't yet be said
To haunt them) and with the fact
That the rocks and trees

And clouds informed by
Vegetative souls, or else—
In the rocks' case—hard,

Cold epitomes
Of their own stoniness, or
Else—in the clouds' case—

All their bright or dark
Occlusive dispositions,
Could cast such strong or

Such lively shadows:
For their strange fragility,
The apparent life

Of their visual
Substances, they might pass for
True apparitions.

But as the child grew
Older she came to reserve
The privilege of

Hanging on to one
Exception to all this (it
Remaining so rare

A flash of beauty):
The shadow a butterfly
Lays so gently on

A leaf, not haunting
It but quickening the life
Of its surface,

Even as it so
Weightlessly brushes it with
Alien darkness.

GHOSTS

When carrying a candle upstairs to light
The way to bed, you suddenly saw in one
    Of the darker corners a touch of
    Visual presence, or a flash of some

Uncreaturely breathing, a whisper of scent,
A whiff of language sighed or sworn or muttered—
    Or when the thinnest finger of cold,
    Bony and light and felt not as a chill

But as if something beyond the realm of heat
And cold had suddenly occupied something
    Not quite like space nearby and clutched at
    Your consciousness as you passed through a draught

In an old British or Northeastern house—that
Is the sort of where and when they appeared in
    (Because they were in hiding there) as
    The faint early light of reason began

To sift into the way things are. After that
What knowledge was, what was meant by "evidence,"
    Changed the ground rules and everything was
    Playing a very different ball game:

Where did they go for safety then—where could they
Lurk among curtains blown by the night wind, or
    Feel welcomed by a house with a sick
    Child lying in a shaded room upstairs—

But in the households where Ignorance, Fear and
Lack of Imagination keep their ménage
    À trois, and literal mindedness
    Governs them all, the air is thick with ghosts,

The world outside creaks and flaps on windless nights,
Banshees shriek in bogs and improbably gowned
      Females flicker across darkened lawns
    For those who cannot tell a trashy tale

From a great fiction. Only in the story
Strongly and beautifully made can any
      Ghost—Creusa, Aeneas' dead
    Wife, met in the darkened light of burning

Troy, the murdered elder Hamlet flinging his
Accusations along the cold battlements—
      Have any standing, being of one
    Substance with all the real beings in their

Strong—rather than merely tall—tales. In dreams and
Delusions we don't know we are tales ourselves
      Till we awaken; all the truest
    Fables are those we know are fabulous.

THE SPARKLERS

The light and the dark halves of our lives give point to what lies
Beneath their two vast domes, both glimmering with pointedness.
In unloving but ever-devoted return for our
Paying such ungrasping attention, two small Presences—
More intimate than any over-painted prospect, more
Vivid than flowers plucked up by our very noticing—
Pierce through the eyesight of the mind, through the eyesight of the
Heart, deep into the dark treasure-vault hidden behind them.

And seeing either one at its trembling work of endless
Nectaring, or of setting out in its body's window
A beautifully intermittent and unheating light,
Presented with some understanding of the awesome force
Of delicacy, we feel the sight of them both: by day—
By summer day—the hummingbird, the firefly at night.

GLIMPSE OF A SILENCE

I thought I saw a bird
At the edge of my vision
(Eyesight can seem absurd—

A mere outsight, deluding
Itself about the world—
To insight, with its exploding

Invisible revelations.)
Of countless colors, the bird
Was also of many motions.

Was seeing it like hearing
As if at a great distance
Some quiet alien roaring,

The otherwise hidden sound
Of a moment passing?
Or was it the echo, drowned

In silence but audible just
Then, of an inner event
From my forgotten past

Returning like a bit
Of song filling and shaping
The silence following it?

Or, for those in need
Of such visual emblems
(Those whose ears can't read),

A rupture in the rush
Of the world that was theirs,
The picture of a hush.

Some said that (but not I),
When conversation stopped,
An angel had just flown by,

But I was soundly told
By a lady who had been born
In a corner of the old

Double Empire the quip
She had heard as a girl
(It seemed to summon up

A world of duels and bets):
When that moment of silence falls
A lieutenant is paying his debts.

Yet, demystifying aside,
Was I not, myself, at the edge
Of my vision and at the wide

End of what utterly
Intruded on the threshold
Between my world and me?

The half-known angel of
My own quick passage through
The realm where what's above

Meets what's below in one
Quick, asterisked silence,
A signal one for when,

An overspent shavetail,
I'll be, at the end of things,
Paying up after all.

JANE

I   *Toward the End*

Jane in graying November now on her last
Legs, looking up and around before eating,
As if wary of the presence of her two
Dead sisters, one gone less than two months ago,
The other one for somewhat over a year.
It is not their ghosts she wants to avoid, though
Nor is it in welcome as she slowly turns
Her head and stares at a new kind of nothing.
(The healthiest cats, of course, always delighting
To stare at nothings as well as at somethings
That aren't there.) Is it her own approaching
Death, unimagined, that she turns away from
Food and water, in order to sense it out?
And is her not knowing what it is—not
Being able to conceive that she would end,
Let alone wonder what that might be like—more
Enviable than our own nutty "knowledge"
Of Death, or not? I'm not sure I wish I knew.

II   *After the End*

And, of course, for several weeks thereafter
She would be somehow present—in dark things
Of roughly the right size down on the floor in
Corners, as if lying in that official
Feline position, all paws tucked beneath the
Rest of her, in unwitting reassurance
(For us, naturally, not for herself, who,
Even at the last end, could not be said to
Need any) that she was there: Jane. Yes. Then. There,
Or in some other darkening along low
Surfaces glanced at in passing—a shadow

Of what had been there once and thereby perhaps
The shadow of some other kind of shadow.
But it could perhaps be said that every glimpse
Given us of What-Was-Not-Jane, each present
Absence, whether or not in place of what was
Not there at the end for Jane, pointed toward
Some dark somewhere where our own ends crouched waiting.

•

WHAT'S ON THE WALL

A sudden startling
Glimpse of someone quite unknown
In the mirror in

The bedroom: it *had*—
Given the facts of the room
(He alone in it,

All the angles of
Incidence and reflection
Being what they were.)—

Nonetheless to be
Himself. This had come to be
A familiar

Occurrence. Though what
Was there tonight was his own
Good old   or old had—

Image, now the wall
Behind him in the mirror
Belonged to a strange

Room not his, a wall
That looked as if a painting
Had been hung on it

And later removed.
Not because the usual
Telltale rectangle

Of paler tone like
A shadow of negative
Pallor revealed where

A framed picture of
Something had for years shielded
   That part of the face

Of an innocent
Wall from the daylight
   That so darkens what it falls

Upon. There was no
Such window showing some part
   Of what once had been.

And yet the wall was
Not exactly blank, but full
   Of invisible

Information, and
If he had been a picture
   Himself, some image

On the wall behind
Him there would be its title,
   Telling what he meant,

What he intended,
What his life had been about
   In the end then, and

Perhaps pointing out
To what in the world outside
   The room it applied.

What was it then that
Hung in the blankness of wall
   For no one to see:

A faded map of
What realm or territory
   The ancient domain

Of his earlier
Failed, aspirations, a world
    Quite unrealized?

A battle scene of
The retreat from Whatwherewhen?
    A still life with

Peaches, pears and plums,
Bathed in a delicious light?
    An Old Testament

(Which for him was quite
As good as New) anecdote
    Of a renaming

Of person or place
Involving some pun hidden
    By the translation?

Or (and this never
To be gleefully noticed
    And identified

By historians
Of art) an unreadable
    Self-portrait by Death?

—Questions not to be
Answered in a mirror now.
    Or even on some

Long walkabout back
Into my since-hidden past,
    Let alone into

The bushes of the
Future from which one cannot
    Speak of returning.

VERY EARLY

Are we to say that the knowledge that there
are physical objects comes very early or very late?
　　　　　　　—Wittgenstein, *On Certainty* A 479

It comes when for the first time a frightened
Child is assured that her dream was indeed
Only a dream—that the white fire engine
Screeching through the window of her low room
Whose terrifying presence awakened her,
Screeching, and an end to itself was,
Though not in our high chamber of sense
Immaterial, nor irrelevant
Nor incompetent, but just not *there,* in
The blessedly lower sense that we grasp
The handles of the world with. Who knows what
She knew about whether everything in
The ever-expanding toy chest of stuff
That made up the *out there* was physical
Or not? Or whether what was happening
To part of "what was happening" could mean,
At the age of three years and a few months,
Hadn't come along for her very late
In her young life? Late in her older one,
She could recall the terror and the dream,
The comforts given on awakening,
But not the coming of the knowledge—if
Indeed that had been a time when it came.

TRACES

He must have existed, if only to cover his tracks.
                    —Henry James, "The Birthplace"

"If only to cover his tracks . . ." Or so opined
The pair of keepers of the flame—in this case,
Of the great Author (not that the flame itself
Illuminated too much of the world).
Well, yes, but what if such tracks turn out to be
Only our own, if trudging around the spinney
Of larch trees following imagined tracks
And then, circling again, we encounter just
The ones that we'd made in our search for them?
Would that mean that they'd been just that much more
Cleverly covered—not by our blindness, but
By all the business of our inferences?

But would *that* matter? No: for the better question
Is rather where and when—in all the sprawling
Of all the plenitudes (admittedly dotted
With both the usual and the sudden startling
Poverties) of our deeds and days—would it
Make some serious difference? At noon? midnight?
At home? At some mad place one found oneself
Lost in? But all of this had nothing to do
With what the Author and his Name could mean:
Such an ever-absent Author of awe
Might perhaps be present in all his works,
Though only if one chose to put it that way;

But as for the keepers—was it the questioning
Itself that had been planted in their keeping,
Long before they came to it, by the engines
Of thought? Or, in their quiet, troubled way
Had they begun the perilous backtracking
Toward where their inner light would have become
Hallucinatory? But we are finally
Left in the dark about all that, we who

Could never want any more of inner light than
We need to read by, or to make more vivid
The traces of our deep, remembered, trackless
Darknesses in their various vivid tones.

OUT OF SIGHT, STILL IN MIND

Those who keep dropping
From the world, taking pieces
Of what we have known

As the world with them:
Dropping like fallen soldiers?
Or, as too many

Have said, like the fall
Leaves—and, as might be added,
Like those drupes and pomes

And nuts and berries
At the end of their brief time
Aloft? Or like black

Lumps of anthracite
Sliding down the chute from coal
Delivery trucks

Into the cellars
Of an apartment building?
Or after all like

The soggy gray blobs
Of wet toilet paper flung
From an eleventh

Floor window in that
Same building by wanton boys
Giggling at their mild

Sport as messiness
Descends on unsuspecting
Heads and hats below?

Or like the dropping
Of rain—falling on concrete
Pavements, rapidly

Evaporating
Or disappearing into
The Metropolis

Of drops in a pond
Or puddle, or else falling
Onto a fair field

And being absorbed
By its surface—rain that chills,
Or bathes or lashes

Or caresses, drops
That may sadden or elate
As they seem to rush

Homeward, drops that can
Renew almost anything
At all save themselves.

UNDECIPHERABLE MS. FOUND IN A TIME CAPSULE

Oh, In the old days of storytelling
There would be enough time left to finish
The message—whatever it was—and fling
The bottle overboard before the ship,
Sinking, would pull the bottle under, too;
Or enough strength left to sail alone
A makeshift craft—jerry-built, jury-rigged—
Far enough away from The Last Island
To cast it upon the waters without
Fear of its being returned like the bread
One had always been advised to deal with
That way. Even a totally empty
Bottle would be a message itself,
Whether couched in highest Diction ". . . and I
Only am escaped alone to tell thee"
Or speaking the broadest vernacular
Of wordless images "I, too, was full
Once; I, too, occupied my far Elsewhere."

But none of the waters can be counted
On anymore. The reassuring hold
On marine vastness by its littoral
Boundaries allowed some hope of some small
Corked vessel reaching some sort of a shore,
With someone to find it, to read, to know.
I can remember the comfort that lay
In blue expanses meaningfully wide
And finite both, can remember being
Assured by the gentle authority
Of my scientific father's calming
Words about the atmosphere's laundering,
Almost unlimited, of the smoke, fumes
And automobile exhaust that on one
Bright cold morning in the waning nineteen
Thirties his calm reassurance led me

To look up into the blue sky graced with
Some brushstrokes of the cumulus of fair
Weather. And I saw the famous azure
There not as the color of hope which dry
But heated later learning would lead me
To read it as, but as the hue of Trust
So saturated, so surrounding and
So—blue—that it obviated the need
For anything like Hope. And I recalled

The similar sea, which I trusted, in
Its vast salinity, to sanitize
When I would pee in it hoping to get
That all done and to swirl my swimming trunks
About before the next big breaker called
Out to me to dive through it: all would be
Clean, now and clean then and ever would be . . .

Well, that's over and with no absorbing
Sky like that, no "waters" and, soon enough,
No one who can read the languages one knows,
Not *"Help! Here I am at Lat. Something and*
Long. Something else," but "No help! Here we were,
Our short-lived aeon with its withering
Futures. You who come after everything
We mean in our language by 'after'—you
May know of us that we had nonetheless
To make known what had been with us before
All that—for you and yours—had ever been."

POLICING THE YARD

Picking up what they'd dropped not long before,
They gain a new acquaintance with the ground
That will return to haunt them all the more.

Lost words and deeds, quickly become a bore,
Make for how tedious they will have found
Picking up what they'd dropped so long before.

The more lost buried memories they store
Up in a subsubsubterranean mound
(Those will return to haunt them all) the more

They find themselves returning to the lore
Of returning, keep on sadly trying to expound
—Picking up what they'd dropped so long before—

The meaning of their task, as they explore
The lowly territory all around.
This will return to haunt them   all the more

For its low hopelessness as well as for
All their conclusions being quite unsound.
Picking up what they'd dropped too long before:
That will return to haunt them all the more.

TALES AND FABLES

MONDAY MORNING

Today we're having the windows washed . . .
I think of how such a journal entry
Might have proceeded if written by an
Actual novelist or superb
Epistolarian (known for her acid
Eye, gentle heart and platinum tongue)
Or essayist of an older sort,
All of whom had memorious eyes
And capacious memories for details:
Their "powers of observation" make
Me feel blind to the moment and
Mindless of just what was said or worn.
The true novelist's mandarin prose
Of whatever mode makes up its own
Recordings of what it made take place
On disks themselves made up of years
Of recycled detailed remembrances
That I don't have to draw or write on.
But I'll give the window washers a try.
Let's see: I'll at least remember that
There were three of them, and one came first
To case the joint, as it were, and that
All of them were of medium height,
Slender and dark and that they did
Indeed clean all the windows, inside and
Out, hanging on safety straps
Above the distant ground. That's it.

But my own windows that look out
On the immediate world—the ones
Through which they used to say the soul
Peers out and love comes in—get washed
Only by tears, and what I know
Of what's out there comes in through one
Of the cleaner spots. Their sizes and

Their placement are both meaningless,
And make me wonder about what
I get to see, whether of windows—
And what goes on when they get cleaned
And who said what to whom and who
Did which and with what—or of mirrored
Eyes or imagined minds. So that
In the matter of the men who came
To clean the windows, what could I say?
"If memory serves . . ." but it will not:
And like language itself when at
Its best or even craziest,
Ich dien it will not say—like each
Dutiful Prince of Wales for seven
Centuries—but rather *non*
Serviam, the Adversary's
No way! At the instant of starting up
The engines of noticing, memory—
As full of random holes as any
Uncleaned window is of spots
Of blur and dimming—begins at once
To interfere, and so one's eyes
Brim with forgetting long before
The presence of a pastness, ears
Can't quite recall what they are hearing.
That's all there is to say about
The windows being washed today.

A BALLAD ROMANTICALLY RESTORED

For Paul Fry

Westron wynd when will thou blow,
The small rain down can rain
Christ if my love were in my armes,
And I in my bed againe.

Then up he rose upon the heath
So dry all summer long,
His love lay dreaming, far away—
Nor heard his wearied song,

Nor saw him stride toward the setting sun
Leaving far behind
The blasted east, troubled and plain
Beclouded and unkind,

Nor felt the beat of his anxious heart,
The touch of his distant hand,
As she lay shivering in her bed
In an unpromised land

He gathered up his heavy harp
Whose strings were weak and slack,
And sighing like a dying wind,
He slung it on his back;

He seized his never-flowering staff,
And with a heavy heart
Set out upon the narrow way
Where two paths forked apart

And to the right lay the darkling wood
Which strips of all who enter
Memories of where they had been,
Like leaves plucked down by winter;

And to the left lay the gleaming field
Which hides in its golden floor
The memories of where one is,
What one is headed for.

And straight ahead where the path died out
A steep hill slowly rose,
And at its top a silent spot
Where the air was in repose,

Where no wind blew through his silent harp
Nor thrummed its slackened strings,
Though it plucked the branches of the trees
With thousands of unseen wings.

And when he gained that silent spot
He gazed toward the faraway
And bitterly unpromised land
Where, shivering, she lay.

But saw no more than the prostrate earth
Maimed by occasional hills,
And felt no more than the warm gray air
Whose very silence chills.

And there he called to the wind again
And again he made his plea
Without the sounds of bird or brook
To lend some melody:

Northron wind when will thou sweep
Away the feverish air?
But no wind blew through his silent harp
Nor thrummed the strands of his hair.

Eastern wind when will thou bring
A message from her to me?
But the east wind answered not a word
As it blew from the eastern sea.

Southern wind where hast thou fled
From dale and lake and hill?
O rare is the good wind that blows
No one any ill,
And the knowing wind with a will to do
One well is rarer still

But no wind blew through his silent harp
Nor caused the boughs to moan,
He was left trembling on that hill
Unanswered and alone.

Then down he went and many a mile
He strode along the path,
Heedless of the sweltering sun
And the great rain's wrath.

And now he came to a narrow lake
Girt by a shelf of stone,
Its surface mirrored nothing, its depths
Returned an unwindy moan:

Dark and still are my silent deeps
Hiding all images there
That first alight on my glittering face
Reflecting but empty air

Where she is and how she fares
Cannot be seen from here
As you sit alone on a shelf of stone
And your hope dries into fear.

Could you but hear the talk of the winds
You could not understand:
But know that she lies alone and ill
In an unpromised land.

Alone and ill in a goatherd's hovel
Along a mountain path

Raving with merciless fever and chills,
Racked by the four winds' wrath

Herself unknowing of where you are
Or how she had come to lie
Alone with only a muttering crone
Waiting for her to die.

Call then no more to the deafened winds
And seek no more to know
Where to find her, even in what
Direction you must go.

With never a word in answer then
He knew, by the water's side,
That the paths toward only nowhere,
With emptiness to guide,
Could take him to her who was to die
And never be his bride.

His staff he thrust into the ground
So hard that it nearly brake,
And hung his empty harp on it
And entered the speaking lake,

His heavy heart was like a stone
That pulled him fast below
Where there was no air to call upon
Nor any wind to blow.

She, wasting distantly away,
Unknowing of his end
Sank ever downward toward her own
As each night's shades descend.

And which of them—he in the lake
She in the mountain snow
Was only a shade in the other's dream—
No one can ever know.

Nor whether the four winds had conspired
To breathe both sleepers and
Their mirrored and embracing dreams
Over the slumbering land.

A DRAFT OF LIGHT

We all had to wear hats against the unvarying sun,
　　Of course; but what was more significant,
We'd had to bring with us—along with our freshly prepared
　　Thoughts, wrapped up in the old way—bottled light
To quench any thirst for knowledge that walking through the dry
　　Valley of grayish terebinths and still
Lizards on chunks of fallen Hellenistic masonry
　　Might intensify through the lengthening
Afternoon. Bottled? Well, all the available light, there
　　In that valley uninflected by much
Shade, was barely fit to drink and having to bring our own
　　Along was always part of the bargain.
When the light is too fierce for shadows to blossom in it,
　　Too dry for any specificity,
Too general for distinctness, too literal for truth,
　　What else, after all, can a person do?
Given that to think one's private thoughts of light was
　　Somehow thereby to drink some of the fluid
Light that is at once itself, and what of it is brought forth
　　Again both by all that it makes visible,
And by what those who see and say have ever said of it,
　　As a flower whose name one knows jumps out—
Not merely in its saturated blue but in its changed
　　Look—from the chaos of these petaled things
And those surrounding it. But light keeps one thing in the dark:
　　The matter of its very origins.

Though babble's tall outrageous tower fell, crumbling under
　　The weight of its own presumption, Language
Had a different tale to tell of itself: that it once
　　Contracted to an insignificant
Point which nonetheless contained all the Meaningfulness that
　　There was to be, and then, this being quite
Unbearable, exploded into all the languages,
　　Chunks flying apart in such different

Directions! And then there were only all the languages.
    Likewise with Light before there was the host
Of private lights reflected by each brush, dot, or pixel
    Of all the surfaces of the seen world,
The world as seen. An untold story, this, and for
    The matters of mass and energy we call
Mind, quite immaterial, but not to the substance of
    Our long walk. Quite the other way: our walk—
Yes . . . nearing, but not at, its end, pausing there, just before
    Leaving the valley for the pine forest
Between it and the sea, we stopped to drink what was surely
    Ours by right—we'd carried it along
The whole long way—and long swallows of it now allowed us
    Rightly to claim to know now where we were
Going, rightly, at last, to know where we'd been all along
    And where it was that we had started from.

SETTING OUT FOR THE INNER AS THE OUTER SETS IN

Here is late in the August afternoon;
Now is a point along this unpaved way
Far past where there'd be any more crossroads
To come upon and consider—let alone
A real fork in the path where, shuddering
With power, responsibility and naked
Vulnerability commingled, he
Could really "choose" to head on one new course
Or another—to blow the Horn, or don
The Cape of Good Hope, say. Now, past the point
Midway between the *from* and the far *to,*
The place from which the path can seem to bend
Through some dimension for which there's no new
Coordinate, he can see *from* and *to*
As one, without yet seeing any real
Resemblance at all . . . That way and this,
High road and low, into the outback, then
In front of what is next—a sea of bubbles,
Forest of sorrows, mount of disappointment,
And stretched below it the wide plains inane
Where all is tweedle and all dumb and dee . . .

What is one's own way, after all? At this
Sharp mental point now he can only claim
The right to know that he'll somehow be left—
Taken over by what he'd undertaken—
Upended in just where he'd ended up.

STEEP DECLENSION

The fortune-teller was nonspecific: Will
  I have to fall into some silly well
    Or smash a borrowed car into a wall?

Or fall (as it is often said) quite ill
  And lie, frail as a lowercase letter "l,"
    In bed for many months and then—that's all?

Or shall some medico give me a pill
  To send me out beyond an ultimate pole,
    Darkness invisible under Nothing's pall,

Hmm? Had she warned that when I climbed a hill
  I'd end up deep down in some dreadful hole?
    Or: that I'd dream I lay in some vast hall

All shivering with fear, on a straw tick,
  While vile invaders gathered to attack
    Against the flimsy castle, and the *tock!*

Of the first arrows fell down on its sick
  Defenders at the walls so that the sack
    Of the whole sad town, stuck in the cul-de-sac

Of a barren valley, could then begin
  In earnest. As for me, it first began
    When a huge yet-to-be-invented gun

Boomed out among the hills: the echoing din
  Was ominous. My second cousin Dan
    (Why bring him in? I perhaps might have done

Without him if I'd—well . . .) who made a mess
  Of many things by trying to amass
    A fortune, ended broke and lachrymose

About it after all—(but I digress;
   Let's see . . . well, back to the bad dream) the grass
      Outside the castle wall was wet and gross

With blood and body parts, and all would die
   Within its walls during that dreadful day
      While the wind howled like a stricken doe

Deep in some forest, fading to a sigh
   As if it wanted somehow (but how?) to say
      That I had reaped what I could not yet sow,

Remembered what I'd never known. The dream
   Would stop then; I'd awake and down a dram
      Of Glenwhatever, while an inner drum

Slowly ceased to rumble, and, it would seem,
   Quickly cease to matter (Dan's boyfriend, Sam,
      Suddenly comes to mind just now, for some

Strong, but silly, reason). So, bit by bit
   We come to see that our lives are about
      Paying for what we had not known we'd bought

In our digressions: brandishing its writ
   Of habeas corpus, till Death puts to rout
      The hopes we'd pampered, and the woes we'd wrought.

We've come down to the place where smoldering fear
   Flares up in certainty's consuming fire
      Sparked by the gypsy's mumblings long before,

And crossed thresholds can lead to what is dear
   No longer, but to what is surely dire
      Behind the ultimately closing door.

ATTIC NIGHTS

For Ben Sonnenberg

Heat rises, and in the process
Of Decembering, the attic
Retains some warmth under a roof
Padded thick with unmelted snow.
In the soft light of a lamp strung
To an overhead socket I
Sit remembering familiar
Attic times of afternoons in
Summer, lit by slanted lightspills
Stealing in from low dormers past
Shadowed corners that were often
Overshadowed with promise and
Sometimes with menace,
A time of light that is no more . . .
(—*No more worth mentioning*, Smart-ass
Would add—*than any object of
A tired lament that is no more*)
But here's now that is yet more, and
Now winter nights sang Campion,
Enlarge the number of their hours
That in their appropriately
Contingent illumination
Can make something quite else of
What has been stored, or kept, or left
Here, tokens of the remembered.
(Or of the forgotten? How to
Tell which, not being one of those
Who lived on all the floors below?)
We abandon our moments to
Memory, and/or we hide them
There, for safekeeping, and then like
Most silly and busybodied
Squirrels quite forget we'd done so.
All the objects we pick up and
Shake, unclasp, turn over gently,

Zip clean open or unbutton,
Somehow keep themselves to themselves
Leaving us momentarily
Dwelling among them, dwelling *on*
Them, and yet unable like some
Roman, Aulus Gellius, say,
To send them from Athens home to
Rome for the benefit of his
Kids' future edification.

An Old Milk Bottle

The child who had heard "Grade-A milk"
(As they called it then) spoken of
Thought of a glass of milk cupped in
Both hands on a wintry morning
As the gray-day milk he swallowed
Staring out over rooftops at
The uninteresting, dim sky.
It was as if even night-milk
—Let alone the milk of sunny
Afternoon—needed nothing by
Way of special designation,
But only the milk of absence
And of a certain clarity.

An Etching in a Broken Frame

Probably Dutch, it depicts a
Windmill upon a mount of bones
—What does that mean?—not a strong kite
Or cheerfully flimsy balloon
Sent cloudward after a funeral
Leaving embodied ground behind
But some other mode of matter
Running hand in hand with the wind
Rather than, merely emptied of

It, at best providing a base
For hopeful and energetic
Whirling arms unhurried, wheeling
Arms to draw a static strength from.

The Remains of the Clarinet

—Well, just the bell, really, and we
Hope, not kept in the far worse hope
Of being cleverly used—like
The violin, painted mauve, top
Removed, passed around by the neck
Full of mixed nuts or else serving
As a very silent butler;
The kettledrum, beheaded, now
A planter; the French horn fixed on
A stand, bell up, now a yawning
Ashtray. But this gently flaring
Ebony tube, ringed with metal,
The bell gazing ceilingward and
Resting on an obsolete desk
Dictionary that itself lies
On a dusty table must be
Spared the ravages of cuteness
That would stand some pens and pencils
In it, or conceal a narrow
Bud vase in its base with a few
Sprigs of lily of the valley
Peeking coyly over its rim
Like white ladies on a tower.
I'd want it to stand open and empty,
Like a shell that is both ear and
Mouth at once, speaking of all its
Singing past and of its present
Listening, and then listening
To the silence of what it now
Has still has commandingly to say.

The Cones

Five of them, two a foot long, three
Tiny ones less than the size of
Limes, the large ones those of redwood
And of ponderosa pine, while
The giant sequoia's cones
Look as if they had shriveled from
Abuse of a botanical
Steroid of some sort in order
That they might tower so above
The forest floor they darken so
In their never-to-be-babbling
Overreaching into the high
Fields of light, high high fields of light.

The Pills

Small, gray, crumbling, in the corner
Of a long-abandoned handbag,
Powdering its cracked red leather
Interior with their dust, like
All their kind these pills, we'd hope,
Contain our ills, and if not—since
Their very name contains (in an
Extension of the more common
Sense of the word) them—then at least
With the hidden magic of the
Molecular gematria
Making pharmacology
Do its problematic business.
But what contains *them*—the tiny
Decorative boxes, plastic
Universal brown containers,
Bottles that leave room for rattling,
Indeed, the word *spills* itself—can't
Quite contain the pills within them.
But there is a pile of larger,

Elliptical dark pills lying
Tumbled on the floor alongside
The headless dressmaking dummy.
What lies equally tumbled deep
Within them is even darker.

The Disk

A pearly gray when issued, now
Dark amber, less than a full inch
In diameter, a child's name,
Date of birth and blood type issued
Feb. or March 1941
And come upon now so very
Many decades later here, on
The floor, near no older boxes.
A good-sized poker chip for a
Six-or-so-year-old, though pierced with
A hole for the ball chain hanging
It from so very thin a neck.
Why was it kept? Why was it found??
Why would we look for answers to
Summer's dust now cold on the floor?

A Good Many Letters

Please do not misunderstand: these
Are not ancient correspondence
Tied in ribbons, nor more recent
Typed letters, single-spaced, full of
The nothing of long-concluded
Business, stacked in boxes with
Acorns that some amnesiac
Chipmunk had fruitlessly stored there
Rattling about among them. These
Letters—children's blocks of various
Sizes, smaller anagram chips,

Uppercase letters thirty-six
Point and larger cut from headlines
As if waiting to be pasted
Onto an ax-murderer's taunt—
Graphemes, characters depicting
The invisible contours of spoken
Sounds. Yet each of them is possessed
By that spirit of *From . . . to . . .* that
Marks the other kind of letter,
Every atom of inscribing
Speaking as if in the voice it
Can only produce when joined with
What the other letters say; or
Characters, say, in some story,
The characters of each of them
Revealing themselves slowly in
Silent concert with the others.
All these letters scattered across
An old, netless, legless, Ping-Pong
Table lying on the floor, full
Of the rich possibilities
That recombination can breed
Packed into the seeds of light by
Which writing illuminates not
Only itself but warms winter
Darkness, cold with meaninglessness.

BEING STUNG BY A BEE ON
THE LEXINGTON AVENUE LOCAL

Ouch! etcetera
Aside, and then likewise the
Conclusion that I

Had indeed not been
Stabbed in the left shoulder with
A knitting needle

By some demented
Wretch whose misery I'd be
Momentarily

Too angry to spare
Any real sympathy for
(Though I knew too well

Life had undone so
Many) sitting in the jammed
Car heading uptown

Through the acutely
Nonrural subway tunnel:
Said conclusion drawn

From a subsequent
Nonmechanical humming
In my ear accompanied

By an actual glimpse
Of the creature who would not
Live long buzzing off,

As it were and as
A matter of fact as well—
What some idiot

Of the literal
Might mean by *rus in urbe* . . .
All of those aside,

It was only weeks
After that I realized
That the very (most

Nonliteral) point
Of the sting was that the thought
Buzzed through my mind some

Days later that I
Was as one who, once stung by
A gold-banded

Bee in a fable,
Might have thereupon acquired
As a gift—not from

Apollo himself,
But from one of his nine girls—
A peculiar kind

Of wisdom: but of
Which sort, and from which of them—
Which of the Muses—

Let alone what tied
That bunch to that misplaced bee
(Poor lost bee! I had

No anger for her
As I might have had for the
Knitting-needle nut)

And what deep cosmic
Questions had hung on this I
Could not imagine.

But although with no
Gift nor Muses nor indeed
An available

Apollo, I would
Come to conclude that even
The subsequent brief

Sting of the sudden
Awareness of them and their
Moot irrelevance

Was as much of a
Gift from those nine sisters as
Is ever given.

STATIONARY BICYCLE

As you go "by" you can see them
All there in their overalls, straw
Hats and red bandannas on their
Far from red necks, singing, as they
Labor, some of the pure versions
Of the songs we'd heard in childhood.
Later on you realize with
Something like chagrin—regret?—that
They were gathering pressed flowers.

This is one of those occasions
At which you can look around, look
Out at what you have been passing
Through some vehicular window
Only by looking in—into
Your own looking itself—and
Now is when the most distant trees
Can speed on by, quickly noticed,
But without releasing any
Sparks of particularity
While what ordinarily would
Be the all-too-evanescent
Glimpses of what is going on
Very nearby take a kind of
Forever to unfold themselves.

But you had been going downhill
For so long that all memory
Of the summit, and surely of
What an ascent must be like, had
Receded long ago, behind
Even the bushes of hearsay.
Onward can get to be upward
Enough, as if all altitude
Were part of the same old fable

Bred in the fact that it is our
Nature to walk vertically
And as if one could finally
Tire of telling it yet once more,
While the same old fact of getting
Up each day remains a relic
Of some construction of habit
And belief, one comes to feel that
It must not become a fetish.

You see, by the light of the lamp
Standing in the otherwise dark
Corner, the much wider light of
One of those growingly golden
Afternoons when on an earnest
Yet slow and casual amble
Down the avenue along which
You look mainly straight ahead, you
Turn, at an odd-numbered side street,
The corner onto another
Language where the world is unlike
The one you've just wandered out of
Because anything you now could
Say of it would be so different.
If thought tripped over some curbstone
There, might that have been avoided
If the word for "curbstone" were the
Same as in the older language
Of the avenues? But you would
Have gone too far eastward before
Something like this could have mattered.

Here we go again!—but is that
The right way to put it when the
World outside you remains unchanged
Whether you stop now or start or
Keep on going or keep being
Stopped?—Well (puff! puff!—it's hard going
"Uphill" at the moment) I guess

It is: the lesson learned about
The effort needed to keep being
Here, now, and not changing any
Of the spatial coordinates
Over time, but simply to keep
Clinging to the unchanging ones.

Going this kind of pure somewhere
Must mean something like our going
On being (whatever being
Is, whatever the predicate
Of "being" is) in whatever
Kind of world the case may be,
Whatever its continuing
Sends invisibly by us, to left
Or right, as you keep pedaling

And so round and round it goes.

WHEN WE WENT UP

The earliest hills: those were the ones we climbed
In early groups. A few kids, going up
There just to go up there, might find out what
There would be, once up there, to do about it.
This was all vague and full of pure delight.

The next thing was, when older, to get up
To the top by myself and pause, breathing in
The satisfaction as I would look around
For that important sample of what the world
Felt like even from some small elevation.

Then older still, up something more impressive
And taxing, in the almost classic way:
Having to get up there in order to grasp—
As Petrarch put it—"its true height" along
With some trusted companion, and some book.

Years later one would go up there alone
Again, this time in a solitariness
If not self-knowing, then at least self conscious
In quest of the prospect rather than whatever
Accomplishing the ascent itself might mean—

Old enough now so that the years behind one
Stretched back along a plain fully as wide
As the broad field of years one's inner eye,
Remembering, looked back on as one's own
And certainly, by now no longer young

Enough "to overlook the world as if
Time and Nature poured their treasures at
Our feet," nor, like the pushed pawn Alice, see
From a slight eminence the chessboard world
As, before, it had never been to be in . . .

Now, in a purer solitude, up we go
For a far more revisionary view
No longer framed in moments still and vast
But one in which spatial *before* dissolves
Into time's usual *after what's right now*:

Painterly layers of more distant clouds
The growing abstraction of near-distant peaks
The visual shiver when we project ourselves
Upon them from the distance where we stand
To a cold loneliness before returning

To the warm homeliness of solitude
Once more. And after that, again with others
Up there—some family perhaps—to whom
I would point out, point toward, a promised future
—Not its particular locus, form, extent,

Not a mere piece of no-man's-land: instead
The very thought of a futurity
That could be counted on might be enough.
The places I saw from the head of that
High Pisgah, my foot on a rock, were those

Into which I would never be allowed
(By whom? By what?—Reality itself)
To enter. Then, and only after that
The final climb—not the ascent itself
(Having been to the top so many times)—

But the last state of being there: then staring
Up and down, gazing around and out
Would show—But what? One's own near-distant form
Seen from the rear, say? Nothing? A burned land?
A flooded one? Swirling vapors? What?—whatever

It was, it was a world beyond the sight
Of the mere visionary, and not rumored of
In some old chronicles of crazy heights—

Of my own old Mount Blank and North Rock, say, lying
Hidden between some long-neglected pages—

Or whatever hill the youth ascended
Waving a banner with some strange device
Embroidered on it, and if from there the world
Might still lie "all before me," after me
There'll be no world that I could ever know—

And what's a world without knowledge of it?
Well . . . a good question! But somehow, at last,
When one has wearied of particular
Heights, and of the idea of altitude
Itself, a terribly unimportant one.

DR. JOHNSON'S FABLE

from a few ms. lines noted by Boswell, 20 April 1773

In the garden of a palace
   Dusk collected on the green,
     Deepening it
As the blackness quite took over.

Lying on a leaf a waiting
   Firefly looked out across
     Terraces and
Borders toward an upper window

Through whose half-drawn curtains could be
   Seen a candle steadily
     Through the failing
Daylight burning, seeing which the

Modest insect had bewailed the
   "Littleness of his own light"
     Till another
Wiser glowworm by him whispered

Wait a little: it will soon be
   Dark, the candle then will seem
     To be flaring
Up into some higher brightness,

Till in cool illumination
   Flashing inner and unseen
     There will come a
Sudden understanding then of

What it means to have "outlasted
   Many of these glaring lights
     Which are only
Brighter as they haste to nothing."

TYPING LESSON: A LITTLE FABLE

The quick, brown fox jumps over the lazy dog

They (whoever "they" are) say
That there is always more
Than just one way
To skin a cat,
Or scamper quickly, like a hungry rat
Right through the subset of the integers—a bore
To demonstrate this on the spot—
But its truth is revealed
Here on this wintry field
When, like a shot
(As "they" say), and
—As if at some stern but unheard command—
Over the lazy fox
Jumps the quick, brown dog
As if hurdling a scrawny-looking log
And unaware of any lurking paradox.
OK. But then what?
Well, the slow fox yawns again
And looks around—but not
At where the dog has gone; but then
The overeager hound,
Tumbling heels over head
Scampers about till he has found
A bright green Frisbee lying there instead.
OK for the doggy, I guess
And as for the alphabet,
OK, too, yet
Represented no less
Well than it was before, in a remix
Of the old twenty-six.
(With some repeated—paddingly, I must confess.)
"Were there an umpire whose decision
Could not be challenged—" fox maintains
(Still up to his old tricks)

I'd win the point of the entire revision"
   But "Point not taken," dog explains
      Refusing to defer
To foxy casuistry (and you and I
     Would probably concur)
"There is no winner here, for whether foxes fly
  Over recumbent dogs, or quite
  The opposite, all but a few
  Downright and, alas, upright
  Proverbs can be reversified.
      Yet that aside,
   Wiser, and *semper fi,*
  It is the dog always, who
Remains more than proverbially true."
  Let sleeping foxes lie.

GETTING IT RIGHT

Allegories on the banks of the Nile were all
   Greek ones, whether with jaws that appeared to
Grin or with figurative reptilian eyes
   Dropping the proverbially phony
Tears onto the unblaming, literal mudbank.
   They made their way invisibly among
The native crocodiles they were so very much
   Unlike, through the slow water unperturbed.
Mrs. Porpalam (the mockers got it backward),
   Who first told us of the allegories
And other species of wild, anomalous life,
   Got it right, herself: so that when we round
Purgatories poking out into the pure sea,
   Cheerful under full sail, or undo the
Prosthetic fallacy by turning the weather
   Inside out and finding everybody's
Feelings stored in it we can thereby reaffirm
   The self-preserving instinct of the Word
To home in on any port in a storm. And once
   Landing upon some particular one,
Being surprised by the innocence and beauty
   Of the inhabitants, their bright clothing,
And firm, cheerful seriousness. The Word
   In question, sojourning there, would give up
Waiting to be rescued after a while and go
   Native, and the precise, melodious
Dialect of the place would claim it. On some warm
   Summer evening it would be welcomed
Among the parts of speech there, and until
   The dawn broke it would dance and dance and dance
With beautiful strange words of unknown origin
   With which, as to the place, it would belong,
Its living there—and this the mockers would never
   Understand—thoroughly appropriate.

FROM THE NOTES OF A TRAVELER

In the mountainous northern portion
Of X—there is a valley quite inaccessible
From adjacent ones, because of an earthquake
And subsequent rock slides. It has
Been so for several hundred years. The village
Culture of this valley is quite like that
Of neighboring ones—the language the same,
Save for the preservation of a few older
Word forms that changed elsewhere
Perhaps because of the influence of travelers' dialects.

But early twentieth-century explorers
All reported the same strange event:
During the course of all ordinary days—
As well as in the interstices of the ceremonial
Occasions on consecrated ones—a man,
Woman or child of the village might be observed
In brief conversational exchanges with one
Or more listeners. The speaker
Would tell some sort of story, marked
By significant, or perhaps merely structural,
Pauses. These little narratives,
Sometimes very brief, sometimes going
On for several minutes, each concluded in
A prominently framed and significantly
Delivered final utterance.

At which almost immediately—with the quickness
Of response which the explorers were, in their
Own societies, accustomed to on the part
Of those being told a joke—

The listeners would silently weep.
And then stop,
And often, then perhaps catching another's eyes,
Might start, as with renewed vigor,
To weep again. It has not yet been determined
What other aberrations accompany this one, in this valley.

FIDDLING AROUND

EMERITUS FACULTIES

He had stepped out into the bare cold yard,
Struck with the suddenness of silence, fearing
That he could yet grow far more hard
    Of hearing;

He shuddered and then turned his gaze aloft,
Hoping for something more but, being
Bathed in a milder light, his eyes felt soft
    Of seeing;

Where the wind shook him, waiting at the rim
Of darkening there, almost jelling
The winter air within, he was left dim
    Of smelling;

Spicing the faithful pie to no avail
Or carefully and dutifully basting
The hopeful roast likewise, when all is pale
    Of tasting,

He touched his own head from within, to prowl
The precincts of thought; then thought, congealing,
Left him not numb, but only rather foul
    Of feeling,

His begging cup each year remaining full
Of less and less from unforgiving
Nature, though he not quite yet terminal
    Of living.

FIDDLE-FADDLE

*I, too, dislike it: there are things that are
important beyond all this fiddle.*
           —M. Moore

Well, all *that* fiddle perhaps. But not this
   sublime faddle, far more important

than whatever "this fiddle" might have been
   (although granted not the resonant

machine of spruce and maple that we need
   to hear certain kinds of the truth with).

"Fiddle" can sound like something having a
   silly middle and thereby of use

for crumpling knowledge—work delighted in,
   devout attention—into a ball

and in some slight annoyance (but not to
   everyone's) tossing it away and

(worse!) averting one's gaze from "fiddle's" dark
   shadow, following it doggedly:

"faddle"—not a past tense of the verb we
   have been fiddling with but rather a

residue of all that business of strings, strings
   bowed and tickled and pinched and plucked,

all that fiddling to which Nero's Rome burned,
   they said, and to which the high walls of

Amphion's Thebes rose as its stones took wing
   settling down into where they belonged—

the faddle of life's rhythms of decay
   and reconstruction once the fiddle's

flying and sighing intonations shape
   all that faddle in its final form

well, then the death of all that's "important"
   incident to the fiddler's own death

—the body, the mind, with their pains and woes,
   their cares and delights, their assessments

of what matters most, all fled—the faddle
   will settle down in its newly found

place in existence, played and playing, sung
   and singing, ever shaping anew

the sounds of what is seen the lights and shades
   of what is heard, and thereby giving

some previously inconceivable
   new meaning to importance itself.

FOR "FIDDLE-DE-DEE"

"What's the French for fiddle-de-dee?" "Fiddle-de-dee's not English,"
Alice replied gravely. "Who ever said it was?" said the Red Queen . . .

What's the French for "fiddle-de-dee"?
But "fiddle-de-dee's not English" (we
Learn from Alice, and must agree).
The "Fiddle" we know, but what's from "Dee"?
Le chat assis in an English tree?

—Well, what's the French for "fiddle-de-dench"?
(That is to say, for "monkey wrench")
—*Once in the works, it produced a stench.*

What's the Greek for "fiddle-de-dex"?
(That is to say, for "Brekekekex)
—*The frog-prince turned out to be great at sex.*

What's the Erse for "fiddle-de-derse"?
(That is to say, for "violent curse"?)
—*Bad cess to you for your English verse!*

What's the Malay for "fiddle-de-day"?
(That is to say, for "That is to say . . .")
— *. . . [There are no true synonyms, anyway . . .]*

What's the Pali for "fiddle-de-dally"?
(That is to say, for "Silicon Valley")
—*Maya deceives you: the Nasdaq won't rally.*

What's the Norwegian for "fiddle-de-degian"?
(That is to say, for "His name is Legion")
—*This aquavit's known in every region.*

What's the Punjabi for "fiddle-de-dabi"?
(That is to say, for "crucifer lobby")
—*They asked for dal but were sent kohlrabi.*

What's the Dutch for "fiddle-de-Dutch"?
(That is to say, for "overmuch")
—*Pea soup and burghers and tulips and such.*

What's the Farsi for "fiddle-de-darsi?"
(That is to say for "devote yourself"—*"darsi"*
In Italian—the Irish would spell it "D'Arcy").

Well, what's the Italian for "fiddle-de-dallion"?
(That is to say, for "spotted stallion")
—*It makes him more randy to munch on a scallion.*

Having made so free with "fiddle-de-dee,"
What's to become now of "fiddle-de-dum"?
—*I think I know. But the word's still mum.*

NO FIDDLING

From the bandstand on
Summer afternoons would come
The non-bowing of

Clarinets sitting
In for violins and the
Brazen assertions

Of the trumpeting,
The heartbeats of drum,
Saxophoned regrets,

All but drowned at last
In the power and fury
Of the deeper brass:

Then the collected
Composure of the softly
Evaded cadence,

A dying moment
Of a lastingness thenceforth
Ever not to be.

SECOND FIDDLE

Fiddle-de-dee, fiddle-de-dee,
The fly has married the bumblebee
Then down to fiddle-de-gee
Then up again to fiddle-de-ay
And way up there to fiddle-de-eeeeeeeeeeeeee—
Which is the way to play.
Is this some kind of boring riddle
Or
Is it that I am the cat and the fiddle?
Both—and more:
Hey diddle bloody diddle
Indeed!— And no, I'm not Stéphane Grappelli,
Nor Joseph Szigeti, the Fiddler of Dooney,
Nor the accomplished busker outside the local deli,
But I'm monumentally looney
If only because the improbable astronomical event
A certain cow was said to jump over,
Instead of munching her clover,
Has become so central to my discontent.
Io sono ammalato
And hearing my own most unmellow
Buzzing yet stingless *sul ponticello*
And watching the dizzying bounce of my *spiccato*
Turns my poor head nightly.

But the centrality I mentioned, of that moon:
The little dog (he was a brown Norfolk terrier, if I remember rightly)
Didn't exactly laugh at it, mind you, but rather lightly
Barked: at it, at the cow, at the cat horsehairing away at the catgut,
    at the song
They were in, and all so perplexed by, for so long:
Were they jailed in it or created by and out of it?
But enough of that. I return to the moon,
Reminded in so doing that (and I have no doubt of it)
Once in a green moon,

Which comes about sometime in early—*that's right!*—June,
This sort of thing has been known to occur:
As in a bad joke,
The dish broke—
Not into pieces but, as it were,
Keeping its physical, if not its moral, integrity—
Into the place where silverware
In its soft brown bed of treated cloth lay there
In its trustful tranquility,
And rummaging through a pile
Of mismatched pieces (whispering all the while
The sort of promises that empty bowls
Are full of) persuaded the silly spoon
(They were poles
Apart in knowledge of the world, the sky, the sun, the moon
The cow had overjumped) to run away
With him and children sing about it to this very day
Unseeing of the darker side of what they sing and say,
And all that I have always known about the games they play.

FIRST MUSIC LESSON

I   *E G B D F*

Every Good Boy Deserves Fun—but either
    I wasn't good, or else I didn't know
Fun when I saw it; whereas, in the matter
    Of those four intervening tones, why, that
Came easily as a familiar jingle—
    The way each note sat in its comfy space
Was obvious, and stared one in the *face*—
    But the lines, oh the lines—they were the problem.
Every time I'd try minding my Bs
    And Ds I'd be a third off either way,
Good grief! (but though short-lived, the minor grief
    Was never good); yet minor pleasures would
Buoy up the spirits, say, feathered eighth notes flying
    About or perched on humming wires. A boy
Deserves—
    Unless you were dead,
    Unless you were deaf—
Fun with the key unlocked by the treble clef
    —Which word, of course, I didn't know meant "key."
But French would come much later, with all the musics
    Of language and the languages of music,
With all the later weight fun bore, and what
    Deserving could itself turn out to mean.

II   *Abandoned Strings*

Of course I don't know about every good
    Girl, nor whether you were one, but you must
Have stood as uncomfortably as I there
    Playing—about five years after I was—
That very first of pieces—yours and mine—
    Acutely unmemorable, but alas

So unforgettable, with underlaid
   Words (not for singing!—but for what?), They went
How still—and—cool—be—side—the—pool
   Yet not so but rather shaky and disturbed
On the open e-string whereto the f on *still*
   And—*side* so scrapingly returned, alas
So scrapingly; and never having reached
   That aria, arranged for fiddle in
The first position and piano from
   The Pearl Fishers (and who were *they*?)

That should have come along later that year.
   And there we were, abandoned and abandoning
The task, so scraping and so hot and bothered,
   Alone at last now (Oh, those poor, poor teachers!)
Beside the pool. How really still and cool
   Shadows of leaves along its edge were, darkly
Reflected foliage that had its own
   Kind of depth, and the never-scraping song
Of feathering oars and dipping paddles far
   Ahead in our young lives, let alone gliding
Into our own *petite phrase* in the first
   Movement of Mozart's C-major quartet
(K. 465—and having that matter, too),
   Let alone learning to take stillness
And coolness with the seriousness they came,
   In all our later scrapings, to deserve.

ANOTHER CAUSE FOR WONDER

I wonder who's kissing her now,
I wonder who's showing her how . . .
            —Will Hough and Frank Adams (1909)

But where's her Now: right there next to her *Then?*
And which one? She has two *Then's*, one before
(*"Maybe by then I'll be a good deal more*
Attractive . . ."), one behind (*Oh then! That's when,*
Back in the old days, I would never . . .). How
Gently the English language can allow
A sinuous movement back and forth to mime
The swinging *Then's* of past and future time
With, charmingly between them both, her Now!

MARINE TONGUE TWISTER

On Ocean Avenue she waits
Just outside the Beach Club's gates.
What's she standing around here for?
She sells seashells by the seashore.

"Newly-Cleaned, Gaily Painted and Lacquered
Hen-Lobsters' Carapaces" a placard
Announced from the wall outside her store
(She sells she-shells by the seashore.)

Streaks of sand caress her legs—
The fisherman's daughter we all adore—
From bivalves piled up high in kegs
She shells seashells by the seashore.

With both hands she bends down and dredges
Up cockles and conchs and clams galore;
Her fingers cut from their sharpened edges,
—Sea cells she sells by the she-sore—

With her mortar aimed at the feminists'
Meeting, enraged with shaking fists,
Fighting her War to End All War
She shells she-cells by the she-shore.

The wind salutes her in its song
Accompanied by the breakers' roar;
Both locals and visitors all day long
See shells she sells by the seashore.

OLD SAWS NEWLY SHARPENED

The Girl on the Hill

Gazing into the blue above, beyond her?
Or listening to its distance, she being blind?
Is it that *absence makes the heart grow fonder?*
Or simply that *out of sight is out of mind?*

Above the Fifty-Yard Line

My fingers on the flask are numb,
But one more gulp might make them number.
One addend doesn't make a sum,
One swallow doesn't make a summer.

The Real Story

Necessity's the mother of . . . (Attention,
Please! Let me be literal, but more profound):
It's Mothers that necessitate invention
And not the (usual) other way around.

And the Greatest of These . . .

Last but not least . . . is it the tiny "e"
Thrust in the midst of this last *last* that (see!)
Undoes some empty paradox like *last,*
But yet not last? And, lest we vainly brood
On what at least has lasted in the past,
Will in the end allow us to conclude
How order is outdone by magnitude.

Two Paths

It's a long lane that has no turning—plain
Lesson for young impatience to be learning.
But what's Oblivion? It's a long lane
    That has no turning.

He Who Laughs Last

—Namely, the one who after the Last End
Of all the other people everywhere,
Awakening in all that vacant air,
Heard first his terrified own breathing rend
The fabric of silence. Animal cries that seemed
Once to sound like human ones now screamed
Inaudibly, as if from far too great
A distance. As he stood in the quiet rain
In his lone verticality inane
He heard his laughter, at (he thought) his fate,
Ultimate, like some decreating Word,
Louder than anything he'd ever heard
Before—the loudness of the world's last laugh
Part childish giggle, part ironic hack
(*Hey nonny nonny ha ha ha yak yak!*)
Emptied of tone and meaning like a cough.

MISSING COORDINATES

A stitch in time saves nine

A stitch in time . . . would have to be some kind
   Of time warp (as the talk of sci-
   Fi would put it) that three blind
   Seamstresses with one bad eye
      Among them would be given
      To repair its riven
   Contiguities, the while
   Moments still gazed bewildered at
      The never that

Consumed all or other moments next or last,
      (One barren *now*, no future
        Then or *then* past).
   Are we to think a single suture
Saves 9? Saves 10, 11, 12 . . . and all
The transfinite infinitudes. Time ripped?
      Sutured and zipped?
      A notion to appall
The hidden gods of space; sewn up and scarred?
What would the site be like when it grew hard?
      The thought that it might have *bled*?—
This had Old Chronos with his untold riches
      In stitches.
   (*It only hurts when I laugh*, he said.)

STILL AND YET

Still and *Yet* parted company when they
Moved into the future; the twins oddly
Both named *Before* dashed off variously
Deep into space and time, but still joined back-
To-back, play ever the two-fronted beast.
Whether for sameness, or their mutual
Canceling of opposites, their barren
Congress—with time behind us, space ahead—
Never yields more than the birth of nothing.

Our own enduring?—As if that could mean
Getting anywhere, as if it could mean
Being anywhen—It is ever to
Be to go toward all that will come to be.

A CONFESSION

I think that I shall never see
A proof or theorem due to me.
No engineering student will
Cope with a Hollander integral;
No algebraist have to stoop
To prove that, in a Hollander group—
(Well, anything!) No topologists
Show that a Hollander Loop exists.
Hollander functions? Only when
"Functions" is a verb, and then
Only part of the time. Again,
History will show no occasion
For citing a Hollander equation;
Never will some string theorist claim
That thirteen letters in my name
Determine the number of dimensions
Nor would logicians have intentions
To work for weeks just to outfox
Their friends with Hollander's paradox.
Nor will I share with such ecstatics
The joys of metamathematics:
In fact, I cannot do much more
Than walk through the unopened door
Of truth, or what's a "meta—" for?

FIDGET

Thought frozen in the
Cold March of a dry winter,
His dry eyes regard

Dark grays and fainter
Grays of near fields and far hills
Motionless, his mind

Playing silently
Over and over with his
Worry-beads of words.

FURTHER ESSAYS

PROSAIC TRANSLATION

Odysseus made a good voyage, out to all that stuff then back—
Through all that other stuff—to the hearth and home
And doggy and her you all could call *nostos.*
Going on the *Argo,* too, was also good—a good trip
To have come back from, having gained a lot of valuable experience,
If you know what I mean, to live out your life among your people,
Those still alive living themselves among those still remembered . . .

"I don't know if or when, / I'll ever see again . . .
Dum de dah dah doo dee—da dah dum dum"—well, I really don't: you never
     know
What can happen, and at any moment—see again those thin chimney stacks
With slowly turning fans atop them, poking up above Manhattan rooftops
Where the high wooden water tanks catch the setting sun from across the
     river.
And when will or may I see the scraggly little park
Behind the Museum of Natural History (the "big," or Central, park
Lying a block or so eastward)? Little and filled with little—
Privet, some small sycamores and ginkos, bits of forsythia –
It was my flourishing Garden of Improvisations, so close
To home and containing me closely as no grandly planted place
On the pages of the largest books ever could.
(Yet—and whether "alas," or not—perhaps would.)

The apartment my parents' none too copious
But steady salaries shored up, and the glimpse,
As I approached it on winter evenings, of its dark red brick façade
Patched with reassuring rectangles of light—I loved it more
Than all the later-known, sanctioned elegances
Of palaces and churches, great, merely grand or even gross,
I would come to fancy that I felt "at home" in the contemplation of.
And the small hexagonal cells of white tile on the bathroom floor—
They were more fascinating than Ravenna's tesserae
Of gold and blue, and still are because I can now see them
Again through the old mind's widely traveled eyes, yes.

Better than the long-ennobled Tiber, the recent Hudson, "lordly"
Only in trope; better than the lovely palace at Urbino
That apartment on 79th Street when I was still small enough
To be happy in its scaled-up capaciousness;
Better than Pisgah, Monadnock, Arlo Hill, Mont Sainte-Victoire, I love
The yet-unbuilt-upon Palisades glimpsed after I had awakened
Each morning when the floods of night receded from my local Ararat.

And as for atmosphere, rather than any change of climate
Of the sort that doctors used to recommend
Involving wide sea or high mountain air, I'd want to breathe again
Scents of the nobly varied realms of narrow shops—
Butcher, baker, greengrocer, fishmarket, drugstore-with-soda-fountain,
    dry cleaners—
On Amsterdam and Broadway, which my childhood inhaled to its wonder and
    delight.

FIFTY YEARS AGO

Gazing across the river long ago
At the still uncolonized Palisades
She marked elusive phantoms across the

Face of the yellowing cliffs—here, a fold
Of rock, a passage of darker hue; there,
The slow work of the afternoon sunlight's

Loaded brush filled the near distances with
New presences made of the stuff by which
Old ones were painted. All this kept claiming

The eye's undivided attention, its
Tiny silver hand moving across each
Letter of the book of the visible,

Its index finger tracing holes, contours,
Frail modulations and limits: there was
Nothing really to say to her other

Than *Here, now! With me! See this—it merits*
Your gaze for which I have such high regard!
So that they are grateful to have been spared

All of the usual compensations
And negotiations that the dim facts
Of parallax reasonably demand.

And such matters now quietly moot, they
Separately apprehended the same
Minute event of light across a good

Distance of grass and walks and streaming cars
And, largely, water, as they held their own
Motionlessness, their eyes entwined, like hands.

ROOTING FOR THE YANKEES
An Ode Batting for an Essay

For Harold Bloom

It started before I'd ever seen a game—
A real game: what of baseball I knew then was that
    I could hardly swing a bat
      (And this was tame
    Softball, mind you); and at my
  Weak, and far-too-overhanded hurl
  They'd cry as one "Aw, he throws like a girl";
    I'd drop each easy fly:
  Time on the field contained an age of shame,
    Nine innings of unending blame,
Before the handful that comprised the crowd
      As when (some older guy
  Caught for both teams and umpired, so no balls
  Or called strikes and nobody was allowed
    To bunt) I swung—and this still galls
    Me to report—hard, and connected
  Weakly with a slowly delivered ball
And sent it dribbling a few meager feet away,
    The pitcher thereupon objected,
  His teammates rushing loudly into the fray,
    Once again affronting
  Me with the accusing cry *"NO BUNTING!"*
    (And what *was* bunting, anyway?
    This was, alas, no way to learn
    About it and I'd dread my turn
At bat.) And if some untried geek proposed to play
(Yes, I was always chosen last, needless to say)
The cry went up: *If we take him, you have to take*
  Hollander—I was what we'd call a flake
  Three decades later and still do today.

    Some time before
  I'd even reached that point (and, to be candid,
I didn't have a scrap of any baseball lore—

Teams, leagues, let alone players and positions)
    An older boy demanded
"Who are you for: *the Yankees or the Giants*?"
    Under such conditions
(His pointed finger pierced the very air)
    What could I say? The calm defiance
Of simple candor was beyond me there
    And then on the Upper West
Side of Manhattan (in those years still blessed
With safety, modest comfort, and peace of several sorts)
    And so I couldn't simply say
        Who are they?
(Though guessing this involved the unknown realm of "Sports")
    So there it was: I blurted out
"Yankees" and so it was it came about.
    Was it because the Giants' name
Seemed too literal, and that the more abstract
"Yankees" doodled my memory (of song
If not of story); and seemed *heimlich*, tame.
In any case the choice I never could retract
    Was made in that quick instant, long
        Before two baseballs—field
Of private failure, and the "Baseball" (MLB),
    The "ball game" that would someday be for me
Of summer-long newsworthiness—had been revealed
    In their ironic, joyful, heartbreaking
        Complexity, the same:
        The Only Serious Game.

    So: an unwitting undertaking
(This was no dream, for I sat broad awaking)
Of a commitment then: was it a true
Confession of some strange belief I never knew
    I had? A verbal penny
    Tossed under pressure? Well, in any
Case, led not by some instructive vision
Whose glowing emblems suddenly arose—
Only the stark plain of the Valley of Decision
    Where alone I blindly chose.
        And so it goes . . .

Years later I would come to understand
    More of the lay of the land
    Claimed by the city's three
Persuasions: Brooklyn was easy—not to be
A Dodgers fan was mindless, dumb perversity
  Of the most blustering and empty kind;
    The Bronx, too: that was Yankee territory
Pure and simple; *Queens? In those days?* Never mind—
    But my Manhattan was another story,
        One could go either way,
        Yankees or Giants, and that day
There on the school bus hardly knowing what I meant,
            I went
        One way and not the other,
        A path my younger brother
        Followed following me
Into the older age of baseball cards
    And on into what then would come
With older age yet: disappointments and rewards
    And Knowledge (slugging averages of batters
        And all such matters) . . .

    And moments that now seem to hum
With ceremoniousness: even now I see
        My first day at The Stadium—
        Regarding alternately
    In their half innings two DiMaggii
    From dead behind, glued to my bleacher seat;
    Scanning the buildings just across the street
    From where we lived to see George "Twinkletoes"
Selkirk emerge (the workaday pinch hitter)—those
    Were such mild, faithful days—let alone Joe's
        (DiMaggio's)
Bowling three alleys down from where I bowled one day
At duckpins (upstairs, on Broadway
And 79th above Woolworth's, the five-and-ten).
        I got his autograph, and then
        Lost it, of course, without too much delay . . .

Or hearing, my brother next to me
Nick Etten in 1943
Batting ferociously
Against the sad St. Louis Browns from deep
Inside an Emerson radio
Whose logogram, a golden treble clef, seemed so
Irrelevant, catching the sunlight of the hot
Summer afternoon.
And, all too soon
That next fall, in ninth grade,
A Giant-rooting classmate made
Pronouncements one day about how Mel Ott
Did not
Remove his drooping pitchers fast enough;
My loyalty sustained a new rebuff:
He added with mild scorn, "The Yankees are a rich
Man's ball club." How I burned
With shame at what I thought I'd learned
Depending upon which
Sense of the genitive was seen
To function, and by "a rich man" you mean
Owners, like the beer baron Colonel Ruppert who
Underpaid players as they used to do,
Or the far richer owner who today
Strives to overpay.
Or, deep in the East Bronx the very far-from-rich
Boys I went to high school with, whose club they were . . .
But I should re-inter
Such catalogues of souvenirs, the *Kitsch*
Of dodderers, dog-eared from the get-go.
And yet although
It became clear that being a Giants fan
Went with the easy left-wing politics
With which we got our kicks
Back then, all this began
To lead me to feel guilty, if not base:
(*I* should have been one of them! Alas,
But let it, pass . . .)

All this is way beside the point in any case—
It wasn't all the substances and accidents
    Of pitching, fielding, managing and batters
            And other matters
    That filled the world of MLB, gave sense
    To a child's game grown up of stick and ball
            And thenceforth, for all
That actual stuff: whatever gripped my power to choose,
        That nineteen-thirties day,
        With a strength it would never lose,
    Late soured knowledge leads me now to say
            And to be sure
That I was "for the Yankees" for the pure
    Reason that I had said I was, and may
            It ever be that way.

    The attachment I confirmed myself in when
            So young back then,
        Thereafter would present
        A moral equivalent,
            I now suppose,
    Of patriotism, of religion, (those
        Last refuges . . .). For, *viz.*
        Overcome by his
    Feelings more of betrayal than mere pique
        The deep believer, Fromm, my friend,
        At the exasperating end
        Of a grim, slumping week,
    Failed pitching, injuries, a pennant race
        Slowed down to a dull trot
    Cries out, appalled at the disgrace
    Offered to Gentiles and to Jews
    *"The New York Yankees? They do not
Exist!"* then three days later, still one of the *grex*
    Of old diehards: *The Sporting News*
        Says we're getting that left-
    Handed reliever, the ferocious X"
        (With this his older tone renews
As if his Faith had been recovered from a theft.).

It is with some love and a touch of shame
    That I, ambivalent, proclaim
  Such innocent, wise faith, too, which commands
Me still, at a tight moment in a Yankee game
When someone at the bottom of the order stands
        There in the clutch
  I, who know better than to care that much
      (Ever a sect of one, unbowed),
      Become part of a crowd
      And yet, of course, alone
    Again an eight-year-old and at
          Bat
Trembling, as I await the punitive first stone.

SOME PLAYTHINGS

A trembling brown bird
standing in the high grass turns
out to be a blown

oakleaf after all.
Was the leaf playing bird, or
was it "just" the wind

playing with the leaf?
Was my very noticing
itself at play with

an irregular
frail patch of brown in the cold
April afternoon?

These questions that hang
motionless in the now-stilled
air: what of their

frailty, in the light
of even the most fragile
of problematic

substances like all
these momentary playthings
of recognition?

Questions that are asked
of questions: no less weighty
and lingeringly

dark than the riddles
posed by any apparent
bird or leaf or breath

of wind, instruments
probing what we feel we know
for some kind of truth.

PRETTY AS A PICTURE

A perfect middle distance, wherein
a girl walks gathering flowers and
singing, perhaps of many flowers
together, perhaps of gathering
itself: as if she had been doing
that, just that, over the centuries
somewhere. I see her song but cannot
hear her singing, can hear her bending,
reaching, gently breaking and holding,
but cannot see just what she has picked.

I gather, too, not flowers, but that
the flowers will wither, wherever
they end up, collected or untouched:
peeking over the palindromic
top of a pot on a mantelpiece,
or gazing out around the room all
in their various directions from
the very middle of a table,
or indeed dulled down and dried up like
the recently gleaming goldenrod
one would never pick in any case . . .

But for now, the togethering here
of all the yet-unplucked: girl, flowers,
recessions of landscape and air, the
untrashed, isolate space that is like
an outdoor room, the touch of figure
and ground mutually gracing each
other, all these dancing round and round
and round in a ring of remembrance,
in the shifting partly shaded light
held somewhere between the beholder
and what it was that he had beheld.

MEDITATION ON A LAWN

"All theory, dear friend, is gray . . ."
—Mephistopheles, in *Faust*

The blossoms fall, of course, and leave
All our visible world to the
Most unfruitful and discursive
Totally theoretic green
Speaking for all that can be seen.
And for what that, unseen, occurs.

What of the mellow, warm colors
Trees reveal? when they come to grieve
Over their early fallen spring
Then the ripe crops of outcrying
Color from which we will gather
Sad knowledge of our store of loss
Will have borne fruit in disbelief—

The molding, model-building leaf,
The clinging and insistent moss,
The broadly speculative grass
On which we think of something as
Something else—their time of the year
Claims to be always. Now and here
Greenness is abstractly severe:
Green is as general as gray
And the theoretical three
Gray Fates who yet in this late day,
Rational and silent and warm,
Reign in practice in their sere
Unflowered, fruitless theory
Are gowned as in the uniform
Of General June's green Everywhere.

WEATHER REPORT

All that cold, rainy
Spring the green deepened as it
  Became absorbed in
Itself, quite inattentive
To the busy details and

  Relations among
Them that we have come to call
  "What was going on."
Outside there, under all the
Wide, pervasive gray of sky

  (Which itself did not
Interfere with very much),
  The garden had so
Intensified beyond mere
Coloration that it had

  Become a substance
On which our starved eyes could graze
  With remembrance, hope
And slow pleasure entangled.
That was the good news. But all

  That June we were plagued
With returning rain's dropouts
  Who keep on dropping
In. Uninvited, of course,
But, we must admit, somehow

  Contracted for; they
Pound away at roofs and eaves
  To be more strongly
Acknowledged and admitted
(In the most loud, literal

Sense) though being let
In by being admitted
    To in a far more
Figurative way—well that's
About all they'd be getting.

    We'd hope to avoid
The mindless patter
    That these visitors
Exchange not with each other.
But only direct at us.

    Yet we live right on
The only route from Great There
    To the favored Heres;
They all stop by on their way
Down, outwearing their welcome

    After a moment—
Then we are not just putting
    Up with them all, but
Putting them up, presently
Paying for the green repast

    We felt we'd paid for
In advance with the broad gray,
    With the yellow light
We'd given up, with the soft
Sound of sunlight on the grass.

AT THE YEAR'S END

Now. At the New Year,
   Hope, fragile, and steady Doubt
Do their pas de deux.

THE WAY IT ALL GOES ON

The journals of all the boring mornings:
A most primitive way
Of writing the way it all goes on—
Today and
Today and
Today, below the variations of even the simplest prose,
But we are stuck with it. And the cheap tricks
We would come up with to try to
Break that dreaded and often dreadful rhythm—
Lots of enjambment across the lines
Of waking and sleeping, lying diagonally across
The bed of night: that sort of thing—can't fool
The Cyclemonger, the One who'd really need to be
Fooled for anything to come of it. Nor indeed would
Having dawn break in the middle of a chant of noon, or
A coffee break suddenly occurring just after
Starting lunch, or Scheherazade realigning her cliff-hangers
So as to end well before each Arabian Morning (that
Would be deadly!). The way it all keeps going
Is on the diurnal, mensual and annual
Sorry-go-round, its grinning horses gritting their teeth
At being either oops and down or immobile
(And which was worse?), the smaller children sitting in a "polisht car"—
A varnished car, a phaeton they used to call it—
Coming round and round again with nothing of the one
Fatal fall of the son
Of the sun, whose name stuck to it.
These horses are not those of Helios,
(Today and
Today and
Today), for
If they were, coming round and round at us again
We might say that they'd have to be, as Heraclitus maintained,
Different each time.
But the delight of the still standing child is that each one—

Other-child-bearing or not—announces
Through the puff-and-chirp of the Calliope "Here
I come again!" while one of those others, borne strapped on and clinging
On her first terrified ride on the moving horses
Prays in its own way for that first feel of the slowing-down
Of the whole thing—the carousel,
The surrounding world rushing toward it.

But outside the playground of comparisons and disguises,
The song of the world seems more and more
To have forgotten the words
And all we have are what we might once have called
The stationary horses (with the thin, smooth poles) of the unvarying refrain,
Again and
Again and
Again,
Until what we have all been sentenced to, the full stop.

QUESTION ABOUT AN OLD QUESTION

Ubi sunt qui ante nos in mundo fuere?°

Ubi sunt—not just all those makers of trope
And weavers of figure who, when yet one more
Of their number dies, keep asking without hope
What was so emptily asked so often before;
A darker riddle with no answer looms
In the twilight of knowledge with its fading glow
For those who linger on among the tombs:
Where am I, though—
Ubi sum adhuc qui maneo?°

We all know where it is they've gone, the dead:
Beyond Noplace, far into wide Nowhere.
Where the very adverb "where?," instead
Of inquiring, dissolves in meaningless air;
And Nowhere, that growing vast anterior
Into which everything alive will flow—
"Nowhere!" too easily answers the querier.
Where am I, though—
Ubi sum adhuc qui maneo?

Where's *A*, where's *B*, where's silly *C*, where *D*
The drunk, and poor, dear *E*, the brokenhearted?
Where lusty *F*, where displaced *H*, where *G*?
(We knew the answer long before we started)
But where is I, singer of this refrain
On a sea that shifts as all the others row
Out into nothing, but on which I remain,
Where am I, though—
Ubi sum adhuc qui maneo?

Where am I? *Here* and *there* and, for the time
Being, traveling downward from back *then*

°*Where am I, who yet remain?*

To *now,* then making the too-easy climb
Upward into a future *now* again—
Where? What can that mean? All that's now apparent
Is where it is we all are going to go
Drawn along by a deep, relentless current.
Until then, though . . .
Ubi sum adhuc qui maneo?

BY NATURE

As if hopefulness
Were a kind of natural
Right instead of a

Sort of malady
Most incident to the mind,
We have looked upward

And then down again,
Looked under, and behind, for
Some acknowledgment

Of what it is we
Act as if we'd been promised.
The jack-o'-lantern

Grin of sunrise, noon's
Reasonable demeanor,
Night's apparently

Loving hand drawing
Her dark curtain between us
And what will come next—

These are what we get,
Having by nature both to
Take it and leave it.

The cold sky, having
Come in time to imitate
Our moods, will giggle

Or frown, as it will,
But without the convictions
We believe we have;

The relenting snow
Will yield to the gray green dark
Surface of the land;

The unforgiving
Land will leave us nothing much
To ground our hopes in;

And the water, wide
With possibility and
With desperation

At once, can take back
What was never more than our
Borrowed buoyancy.

Notes

GLIMPSE OF A SILENCE	shavetail: newly commissioned second lieutenant
POLICING THE YARD	policing: military slang for picking up bits of trash
MONDAY MORNING	*ich dien* [I serve]: heraldic device of the Prince of Wales; *non serviam* [I won't serve]: traditionally, Satan to God
A BALLAD ROMANTICALLY RESTORED	The italicized stanza, ca. 1500 or before, was highly praised by modernists as a perfect, compact, and intense poem. It was probably one stanza of a lost ballad.
ATTIC NIGHTS	Aulus Gellius (ca. 125–ca. 180 CE): Roman author of *Noctes Atticae*, a commonplace book full of all sorts of knowledge, reading, and conversation and written mostly while he was in Greece; gematria: alphabetic numerology
GETTING IT RIGHT	Allegories on the banks of the Nile: invoked by Mrs. Malaprop (in Sheridan's *The Rivals*); her palindromic descendent shows up here eight lines further on
FOR "FIDDLE-DE-DEE"	Brekckekex: *Brekekekex ko-ax ko-ax* refrain sung by the chorus of frogs in Aristophanes' play
SECOND FIDDLE	Stéphane Grappelli: Parisian jazz violinist; Joseph Szigeti: a great classical one; Fiddler of Dooney: personage in a lyric by Yeats
FIRST MUSIC LESSON	*Every Good Boy Deserves Fun*: mnemonic for the notes marked by the lines of the treble clef
PROSAIC TRANSLATION	Joachim Du Bellay's celebrated sonnet, "*Heureux qui, comme Ulysse, a fait un beau voyage, / Ou comme cestuy-là, qui conquit la toison.*

FIFTY YEARS AGO   Palisades: on the New Jersey side of the Hudson, facing Manhattan; after World War II massive high-rises were built atop them

QUESTION ABOUT AN   *Ubi sunt qui ante nos in mundo fuere?*: "Where
OLD QUESTION   are those who were in the world before we were?" from "Gaudeamus Igitur," the neo-Latin students' song

Acknowledgments

The American Scholar: "Another Cause for Wonder," "Jane," "Typing Lesson: A Little Fable," "What's on the Wall"

The Atlantic Monthly: "Emeritus Faculties"

Denver Quarterly: "Dr. Johnson's Fable"

The Georgia Review: "First Music Lesson," "Ghosts"

The Hopkins Review: "A Ballad Romantically Restored," "Being Stung by a Bee on the Lexington Avenue Local," "Setting Out for the Inner as the Outer Sets In"

Hotel Amerika: For "Fiddle-De-Dee," "Missing Coordinates"

The Hudson Review: "Prosaic Translation," "Pretty as a Picture"

The Kenyon Review: "Steep Declension"

Literary Imagination: "Glimpse of a Silence," "Old Saws Newly Sharpened"

The New Criterion: "Fiddle-Faddle"

The New Republic: "Policing the Yard," "Question about an Old Question"

The New York Review of Books: "By Nature"

The New York Times: [Op-Ed] "Meditation on a Lawn"

The New Yorker: "Fidget," "Monday Morning"

Partisan Review: "From the Notes of a Traveler"

Ploughshares: "A Draft of Light"

Raritan: "Attic Nights," "Out of Sight, Still in Mind," "Some Playthings," "Stationary Bicycle," "Very Early"

TLS: "A Ghost Story," "Marine Tongue Twister"

Washington Square: "The Sparklers"

The Yale Review: "Fifty Years Ago," "Getting It Right," "Rooting for the Yankees"

"The Outcasts" first appeared in a volume called *Chance of a Ghost,* ed. Gloria Vando and Phil Miller (Kansas City, Mo., 2005).

"Second Fiddle" appeared under a different title in *The Salt Companion to Harold Bloom,* ed. Graham Allen and Roy Sellars (Cambridge, 2007).

A Note About the Author

JOHN HOLLANDER is the author of eighteen collections of poetry and eight books of criticism, and he has also edited several poetry anthologies. In 1990 he received a MacArthur Fellowship. He has taught at Connecticut College, Hunter College, and the Graduate Center at CUNY. He is currently Sterling Professor Emeritus of English at Yale and lives in Woodbridge, Connecticut.

A Note on the Type

This book was set in Caledonia, a typeface designed by W. A. Dwiggins (1880–1956). It belongs to the family of printing types called "modern face" by printers—a term used to mark the change in style of the type letters that occurred around 1800. Caledonia borders on the general design of Scotch Roman, but it is more freely drawn than that letter. This version of Caledonia was adapted by David Berlow in 1979.

Composed by Stratford, a TexTech business,
Brattleboro, Vermont
Printed and bound by Thomson-Shore, Inc.,
Dexter, Michigan
Designed by Anthea Lingeman